Real Science-4

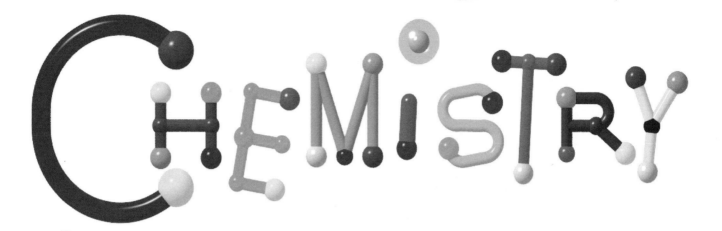

CHEMISTRY

Level II

Teacher's Manual

Dr. R. W. Keller

RealScience
4
KIds

Cover design: David Keller
Opening page: David Keller, Rebecca Keller
Illustrations: Rebecca Keller

Copyright © 2007 Gravitas Publications, Inc.

Real Science-4-Kids: Chemistry Level II-Teacher's manual

ISBN: 9780976509783

Published by Gravitas Publications, Inc.
P.O. Box 4790
Albuquerque, NM 87196-4790

Printed in the United States

GRAVITAS
PUBLICATIONS INC

To the teacher (a note from the author)

In this teacher's manual you will find all of the answers to the Study Questions and Practice Problems in the Chemistry Level II Student Text. You will also find a "Suggested Experiment" for each chapter.

In the student laboratory workbook, I encourage the students to design their own experiments. I want students to learn how to create new scientific ideas and the only way to get them to do that is to encourage them to try. Anyone can find a number of science "experiments" or recipes to follow in a variety of science lab textbooks and on the internet. But the point of scientific investigation is to discover what is not yet known and some of the most exciting science is discovered by scientists creating new ways to do new things that no one has tried before.

It is important for teachers to give students the freedom to think for themselves and, within reason, to experiment with ideas that you, the teacher, may know won't work. If your student decides to use bubble gum instead of masking tape to attach a test tube to a jar, let them try. It may work beautifully or it may fail and ruin the whole experiment, but at least they tried and in the end they may know quite a lot more about bubble gum than they would have without trying. It is fine to guide them in order to help them find better ways to conduct scientific experiments such as the use of controls, but don't get overly concerned that they do the experiment "right." The process of learning through *experimentation* is the most important aspect of these experiments.

Also, as much as possible, answer their questions with more questions. Use lots of "How," "Why," and "What" questions.

Student : "How do I get the test tube to stick to the inside of the jar containing water?"

Teacher: "How would you do it?"

Student: "I think I'd like to use bubble gum."

Teacher: "Why do you think that will work?"

Student: "Well, because bubble gum is still sticky inside my mouth and my mouth has water in it, so it should stick in water."

Their answers may surprise you.

Most importantly - be safe and have fun!

Rebecca W. Keller, Ph.D.

Laboratory Safety

Most of these experiments use household items. However, some items, such as iodine, are extremely poisonous. Extra care should be taken while working with all chemicals in this series of experiments. The following are some general laboratory precautions that should be applied to the home laboratory:

Never put things in your mouth without explicit instructions to do so. This means that food items should not be eaten unless tasting or eating is part of the experiment.

Use safety glasses while using glass objects or strong chemicals such as bleach.

Wash hands before and after handling chemicals.

Use adult supervision while working with iodine and while conducting any step requiring a stove.

Contents

Text reading time .... 2 hours

Experiment time .... 2-3 hours

Suggested Materials :
    any packaged materials
    that have the salt content
    listed on the side of the
    box in milligrams (mg)

ANSWERS TO STUDY QUESTIONS

1. protons, neutrons, and electrons. Protons have a positive (+) charge and electrons have a negative (-) charge. Neutrons have no charge.

2. 150

3. 54 amu

4. a. chlorine Cl
    b. carbon C
    c. lithium Li
    d. nitrogen N
    e. mercury Hg

5. atomic number 9, fluorine; atomic number 17, chlorine; atomic number 35, bromine

6. atomic number 10, neon; atomic number 36, krypton; atomic number 2, helium; atomic number 18, argon.

7. atomic number 3, lithium; atomic number 11, sodium; atomic number 19, potassium; atomic number 37 rubidium.

8. one mole

9. one mole weighs 10.81 grams, so 3 moles would be: 3 x 10.81 = 32.43 grams.

10. To find how much one mole of ammonia weighs, first look on the periodic chart and find the atomic weight for each atom in the ammonia molecule.

   one mole of nitrogen weighs 14.01 grams
   one mole of hydrogen weighs 1.00 grams

   Next, write down how many of each kind of atom ammonia has.

   ammonia has one (1) nitrogen atom and three (3) hydrogen atoms:

   Now, plug these numbers into an equation where the number of each atom is multiplied by their atomic weight.

   One (1) nitrogen atom times 14.01 grams, plus (+) three (3) hydrogen atoms times 1.001 equals (=) 17.01 grams.

   [(1 N) x (14.01grams)] + [(3 H) x (1.00grams)] = 14.01grams + 3grams = 17.01grams

   one mole of ammonia weighs 17.01 grams.

INSTRUCTIONS FOR EXPERIMENT 1: LOW SODIUM

In this chapter students learned about matter, mass, and moles. The experiment outlined below will help students further explore these concepts.

The student will need to learn dimensional analysis to perform this experiment. A full discussion of dimensional analysis is given in Appendix D. Have the student read Appendix D before doing the experiment.

In this experiment, the student is given a hypothetical request by their family doctor to limit their sodium intake. The limit is expressed in moles. They will discover that all of the food products list the sodium amount in milligrams (mg). Help the student think about how to solve this dilemma.

A "hint" is provided to help the student get started.

If your student gets stuck or frustrated, help them think through the experiment by asking the following questions.

1. What can you call your experiment? What are you trying to find out with this experiment?

2. What is an "objective?" Specifically, what is your objective with this experiment? What did the doctor request?

3. What is a "hypothesis?" What foods do you think you may or may not be able to eat?

4. How would you write the steps for the experiment? What do you think you should do first?

5. How could you organize the information from the food labels? Can you put the information in a table or a graph? Which information do you think you should look for? What is the "daily recommended allowance?" What is the serving size for each item?

6. How many food items do you think you should check?

7. What if all of the food items have too much sodium? Should you look for other food items? Do you think you could eat less of each?

8. What is a "conclusion?" Did you prove or disprove your hypothesis? How can you tell?

Experiment 1:   Low Sodium

You go to the familiy doctor and he decides to put you on a special diet. He tells you that you have been eating too much sodium. He tells you not to eat more than 0.01 moles of sodium per day. This sounds pretty easy, until you go home and find out that all of the food items list the amount of sodium in mg (milligrams). How do you follow the doctor's orders? Which foods can you eat?

HINTS:

First determine the atomic weight of sodium. It is on the periodic chart and the quantity is given as grams per mole (grams/mole). Record this quantity here   _22.99 grams/mole_

Remember that the atomic weight tells you how many grams of an element are in one mole. But you need to find out how many milligrams are in 0.01 moles. To find out how many milligrams of sodium are in 0.01 moles, first convert grams of sodium in one mole to milligrams of sodium (1000 milligram = 1 grams) in one mole and then mulitply by 0.01 moles. This will give you milligrams of sodium in 0.01 moles.

Do your calculation here:

There are 22.99 grams of sodium in one mole.

22.99 grams (in one mole) x 1000 milligrams/grams = 22990 milligrams (in one mole)

$$\frac{(22.99 \text{ grams}) (1000 \text{ milligrams})}{\text{gram}} = 22990 \text{ milligrams}$$

22990 milligrams/mole x 0.01 moles = 229.9 milligrams

$$\frac{(22990 \text{ mg}) (0.01 \text{ moles})}{\text{mole}} = 229.9 \text{ mg (milligrams)}$$

milligrams (mg) of sodium in 0.01 moles =   *229.9 mg sodium*

Now set up your experiment.

Experiment 1: _What can I eat?_   Date: _____

Objective: _To determine which foods contain less than 0.01 moles of sodium per serving_

Hypothesis: _I will be able to eat cereal, but not peanut butter._

I. List the Materials you need:

MATERIALS

1. Calculation from page 1 of this experiment.
2. Several food item package containers.
3. pen

II. Write out the steps of your experiment in as much detail as possible.

EXPERIMENT

1. _First I will record how much sodium is in 0.01 moles._

2. _Next, I will make a list of several items and record the amount of sodium in each._

3. _I will then compare the amount of sodium in each food item with the limit._

4. _I will determine the food items below the limit and list these as permissible foods._

5.

III. Record your results.

RESULTS

Food Item	Serving size	Sodium (in milligrams)
Raisin Bran cereal	1 cup	350 mg
Nature Valley Granola Bars	2 bars	160 mg
Jiff Peanut Butter	2 Tbsp	150 mg
Chicken of the Sea tuna	2 oz.	250 mg
Baked Beans	1/2 cup	550 mg

Foods that are below 229 mg sodium:

Granola bars - 2 bars, 160 mg sodium

Peanut butter - 2 Tbsp, 150 mg sodium

IV. Discuss your results and write your conclusions.

CONCLUSIONS

If I follow the serving size suggestions for each food item, I will only be allowed to eat the peanut butter

and granola bars.

_____

_____

My hypothesis was incorrect, I am not able to eat the cereal at the suggested serving size.

_____

_____

I can reduce the serving size for the food items with high sodium and still be within the 0.01 mole limit.

I can eat less than 1/4 cup of baked beans, or 1 oz. of tuna, or 1/2 cup of bran cereal.

_____

_____

_____

_____

_____

_____

_____

_____

_____

_____

_____

_____

_____

_____

Text reading time .... 2 hours

Experiment time .... 2-3 hours

Suggested materials :
　　　small colored marshmallows
　　　large marshmallows
　　　gum drops
　　　toothpicks
　　　balloons
　　　modeling clay
　　　flexible straws

Plastic modeling kits can be purchased from several different vendors such as:
　　　Molymod® kits WWW.MOLYMOD.COM.
　　　Darling Models WWW.DARLINGMODELS.COM.
　　　Ward's Natural Science WWW.WARDSSCI.COM

ANSWERS TO STUDY QUESTIONS: PART A

1. The three types of orbitals are "s," "p," and "d."

2.
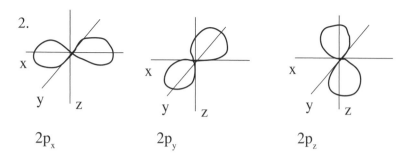

$2p_x$ $2p_y$ $2p_z$

The orbitals are drawn along the labeled axis. The $2p_x$ orbital lies along the x-axis, the $2p_y$ orbital lies along the y-axis and the $2p_z$ orbital lies along the z-axis.

3. $3d_{xy}$, $3d_{xz}$, $3d_{yz}$, $3d_{x^2-y^2}$, $3d_{z^2}$

4. The Pauli Principle states that each orbital can hold at most 2 electrons.

5. The Aufbau Principle states that orbitals must be filled in a particular order.

6. Nitrogen has two electrons in the 1s orbital, two electrons in the 2s orbital and three electrons in the 2p orbitals. Each 2p orbital carries one electron and so each 2p orbital is "half-full."

7. Sodium has a filled neon subshell, with 2 electrons in the 1s orbital, 2 electrons in the 2s orbital, 6 electrons in the 2p orbital. Sodium also has one electron in the 3s orbital. The 3s orbital is "half-full."

8. All of the orbitals for noble gases are filled.

9. The orbitals for the alkali metals have one more electron than its nearest noble gas.

10. The orbitals for the halogens have one fewer electron than its nearest noble gas.

ANSWERS TO STUDY QUESTIONS: PART B

1. When lithium loses an electron it is called a cation.

2. When sodium loses an electron it is called a cation.

3. When chlorine gains an electron it is called an anion.

4. Fluorine gains an electron.

5. Magnesium loses 2 electrons in $MgCl_2$.

6. Two chlorine atoms combine to form the ionic compound $CaCl_2$.

7. Molecular hydrogen (H_2) has a covalent bond.

8. The molecular bonding orbital for molecular hydrogen is called the "sigma 1s squared" orbital ($\sigma_{1s}2$).

9. pi bond

10. sp hybrid orbital [one s-orbital + one p-orbtial]
    sp^2 hybrid orbital [one s-orbital + two p-orbitals]
    sp^3 hybrid orbital [one s-orbital + three p-orbitals]

INSTRUCTIONS FOR EXPERIMENT 2: BUILDING MOLECULES

In this experiment the student will create molecular models. Help the student think about how they could illustrate the different types of bonding and hybrid orbitals for various molecules. They can use any sort of building material they choose.

Plastic molecular modeling kits can be used in place of homemade modeling materials. Several different types of molecular modeling kits are available and can be purchased from a number of different sources [See Suggested Materials].

Help your student think about how they might build a molecular model. Some suggested materials are listed below:

sigma bonds - toothpicks or flexible straws.
pi bonds - flexible straws.
atoms - gum drops, small and large marshmallows.
non-bonding electron pairs - balloons.

If they get stuck, help them think through the problem with the following questions:

1. What would you need to use to model an atom?

2. Do you think you will need to model all of the electrons?

3. How would you model a sigma bond?

4. How would you model a pi bond?

5. What about non-bonding pairs, how could you model those?

6. How could you illustrate an ion?

Experiment 2:   Building Molecules

You need to explain to your mom, dad, younger, or older siblings how molecular bonds are formed. To do this you need to build models so they can understand how atoms combine to form molecular bonds.

Experiment: _Building Molecules_____   Date: _____

Objective: _To use models for understanding how molecular bonding works._____ ._____

Hint: Review Appendix A and carefully study all of the different ways atoms combine to form molecules.

Before you begin collecting items for your models, think about the two different kinds of bonds you need to illustrate (ionic and covalent). What would you need to demonstrate these two types of bonds?

Next, think about the kinds of molecular bonding orbitals for covalent bonds (sigma and pi). How could you build models to demonstrate these?

Finally think about the different kinds of hybrid orbitals (sp, sp^2 sp^3) that form some covalent bonds. What would you need to make models for these?

I. List the Materials you need:

Materials

_toothpicks_____

_small marshmallows_____

_large marshmallows_____

_flexible straws_____

_ballons_____

_____

_____

_____

_____

_____

_____

II. Write out the steps of your experiment in as much detail as possible.
Hint: List the names of molecules you will use to demonstrate (e.g. NaCl, H_2 etc.)

Experiment

1. *After the materials have been collected, I select several molecules to illustrate.*

2. *I will need to illustrate sigma bonds, pi bonds, sp hybrid orbitals, sp^2 hybrid orbitals, and sp^3 hybrid orbitals.*

3. *To illustrate a sigma bond I will model CH_4.*

4. *To illustrate a pi bond I will model CO_2.*

5. *To illustrate an sp hybrid I will model BeH_2. For an sp^2 hybrid I will model BH_3, and for an sp^3 hybrid, I will model CH_4.*

6. *I will use toothpicks for sigma bonds, flexible straws for pi bonds and marshmallows for molecules.*

III. Record your results.

Results

Student's results will vary. Help your student decide how to best record their results. They can use illustrations, or photographs.

_____

_____

_____

_____

_____

_____

_____

_____

_____

_____

_____

IV. Discuss your results and write your conclusions.

CONCLUSIONS

Help the student draw conclusions. How easy (or difficult) was it to build suitable models?
Were they able to explain to friends or family members how bonding works with their models?
What problems did they encounter?

_____

_____

_____

_____

_____

_____

_____

_____

_____

_____

_____

_____

_____

_____

_____

_____

_____

_____

_____

_____

_____

Text reading time .... 1 hour

Experiment time .... 2-3 hours

Suggested materials :
  two small test tubes
  9 V battery
  two strands of insulated copper wire [18 guage]
  salt
  water
  small cup or beaker
  strong tape (such as duct tape)

WARNING

The suggested experiment generates hydrogen gas which is extremely flammable. Please use caution.

ANSWERS TO PRACTICE PROBLEMS

Practice Problem 3.1

2 moles of water decompose into 2 moles of H_2 gas. This means there is a 1:1 ratio. 4 moles of water gives 4 moles of H_2 gas. H_2 has a molecular weight of 2 grams per mole.

$$(4 \text{ moles}) \times (2 \text{ grams} / \text{mole}) = 8 \text{ grams}.$$
(moles cancel)

Practice Problem 3.2

46 grams of sodium is equal to 2 moles of sodium. 2 moles of sodium gives 2 moles of sodium hydroxide. The molecular weight for sodium hydroxide is 40 grams per mole.

$$(2 \text{ moles}) \times (40 \text{ grams/mole}) = 80 \text{ grams}.$$
(moles cancel)

ANSWERS TO STUDY QUESTIONS

1. water, H_2O ; vinegar (acetic acid) $C_2O_2H_4$; baking soda (sodium bicarbonate) $NaHCO_3$

2. (1) $C_2O_2H_4$ + (1) $NaHCO_3$ ----------> (1) $NaC_2O_2H_3$ + (1) CO_2 + (1) H_2O
   acetic acid   sodium bicarbonate   sodium acetate   carbon dioxide   water

3. 6

4. a. $CO + 3 H_2 ---> CH_4 + H_2O$
   b. balanced as is
   c. $C_3H_8 + 5O_2 ---> 3CO_2 + 4H_2O$
   d. $3Mg + N_2 ---> Mg_3N_2$

5. Yes the equation is balanced.

C atoms	H atom	O atoms	----->	C atoms	H atoms	O atoms
6	12	18		6	12	18

INSTRUCTIONS FOR EXPERIMENT 3: MASS MATTERS

In this experiment the students will design an experiment to determine if mass is conserved. Encourage students to develop their own ideas. The questions provided will help students think about how to design their own experiment. A suggested experiment is given. Students can complete the suggested experiment first and then design their own experiment.

Experiment 3: Mass Matters

You need to design and perform an experiment to determine if mass is conserved during a chemical reaction. You can use any experimental approach you choose and the following experimental set up is only a suggestion.

Before you begin and to get you started, ask yourself the following questions:

(1) What chemical reactions am I aware of that produce products that can be collected and/or measured?

baking soda and vinegar react and give off carbon dioxide

vinegar precipitates protein from milk

(2) How would I collect the following types of products: a gas, a solid precipate, a liquid?

an inverted jar or inverted test tube or a balloon could be used to collect a gas.

a solid precipitate can be filtered

a liquid can be collected in a jar.

(3) How would I measure the following types of products if I could collect them: a gas, a solid precipitate, a liquid?

a gas can be measured in a balloon or by displacing a liquid

a solid can be dried and weighed

a liquid can be measured in a measuring cup

Suggested Experiment: Splitting Water

As you know, the chemical formula for water is H_2O. This means that in a single molecule of water there are two hydrogen atoms for every oxygen atom. You can perform a decomposition reaction on water by passing an electric current through a cup full of salt water. The water molecules in the salt water split apart [decompose] into hydrogen gas and oxygen gas. The following set up will allow you to split water and measure the oxygen gas and hydrogen gas that is released. [*Challenge: Why do you need salt in the water?*] [*Answer - to conduct electricity*]

Experiment 3:   *Splitting Water*   Date: _____

Objective: *To split water into hydrogen gas and oxygen gas using an electric current*

Hypothesis: *Because there are two hydrogen atoms for every oxygen atom, we should get*
              twice as much hydrogen gas as oxygen gas.

Materials list: *two small test tubes*
                   9 V battery
                   two strands of plastic coated wire [18 guage]
                   baking soda
                   water
                   cup, beaker, or jar
                   strong tape (such as duct tape)

Figure 1: Suggested Equipment

Experimental set up:

(1) Take the plastic coated wire and cut it into two pieces. With a wire stripper, strip about 4 cm off both ends of both pieces of wire. Make sure you have enough exposed wire to wrap around the battery leads.

(2) Next, fold one end of the wire and tuck it underneath the open end of the test tube. Repeat with the second wire and second test tube. Tape the wire to the outside of the test tube keeping the tucked end inside.

(3) In a separate container add some (1-2 Tbs.) baking soda to some (1-2 cups) warm water. Dissolve the baking soda completely.

(4) Pour the baking soda water into the beaker and fill each test tube with the baking soda water. Carefully invert the test tubes into the water-filled beaker without allowing too much air to rise up into the test tube.

(5) Tape the test tubes to the inside of the beaker along the top edge above the water. Now take the other ends of the wire and attach them to the battery. You should see bubbles beginning to form on the wires under the test tubes. These wires are "electrodes" and the water is split into hydrogen gas on one electrode and oxygen gas on the other electrode. You are now collecting hydrogen gas in one test tube and oxygen gas in the other test tube.

(6) If you want to stop the reaction, disconnect one of the wires from one of the battery terminals.

(7) Try to see if you can determine which electrode is releasing hydrogen gas and which electrode is releasing oxygen gas.

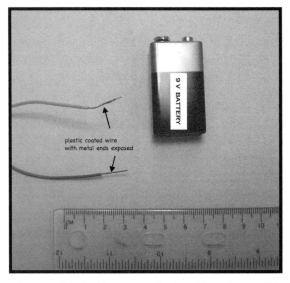

Figure 2: Battery and plastic wire with exposed ends.

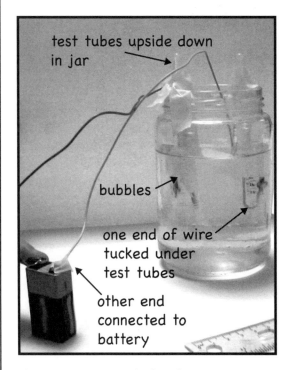

Figure 3: Suggested set up.

This is a fairly straight-forward experiment and should allow students to observe how water is split into hydrogen gas and oxygen gas with each electrode generating a different quantity of bubbles.

Try to help the students "measure" the amount of hydrogen gas and oxygen gas being generated at each electrode. They can do this by first noting the level of water in the inverted test tubes. Marking the level with a water-proof pen and then after a given amount of time, measuring the amount of water remaining. They can measure the amount of water remaining using a ruler and record the quantity in "mm."

They can plot the amount of water left at each terminal for several time points. For example they can collect and plot data for the time vs. millimeters (mm) displaced by the bubbles.

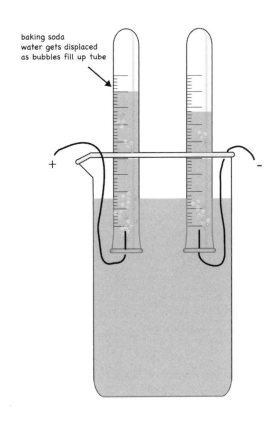

baking soda
water gets displaced
as bubbles fill up tube

Time (sec)	Tube 1(mm)	Tube 2 (mm)
15	2	4
30	5	11
45	9	19
60	12	25
75	15	32
90	17	- emptied tube

Help your students discuss their conclusions. Ask them about what problems they encountered in the experiment, what they would do to fix those problems, and what sources of error they encountered. Ask them if they think they were able to determine which electrode produced hydrogen gas and which electrode produced oxygen gas.

Text reading time .... 2 hours

Experiment time .... 2-3 hours

Suggested materials :
    red cabbage
    distilled water
    ammonia
    vinegar
    baking soda
    eye dropper

ANSWERS TO STUDY QUESTIONS

1. hydrochloric acid, HCl; hydrofluoric acid, HF; acetic acid CH_3COOH.

2. phosphoric acid, H_3PO_4, carbonic acid, H_2CO_3; sulfuric acid, H_2SO_4.

3. An Arrhenius acid releases a proton, H^+, and an Arrhenius base releases an OH^-.

4. Molarity is defined as "moles per liter." Divide the number of moles by liters to find molarity. The symbol for molarity is "M."

    a. 5 moles/ 2 liters = 2.5 M

    b. 2 moles /1 liter = 2 M

    c. 0.5 /1 liter = 0.5 M

    d. 18 grams of HCl = 1 mole HCl. 1 mole /1 liter = 1 M

5. A stong acid or base ionizes more completely than a weak acid or base.

6. pH = 11. It is a base. 1×10^{-11} mol/liter.

7. pH = 1. It is an acid.

8. 1×10^{-6}

9. 1×10^{-9}

Challenge

10. The hydrogen ion concentraion is 1×10^{-7} mol/liter.

     The hydroxyl ion concentration is 1×10^{-11} mol/liter..

     The pOH is 7.

INSTRUCTIONS FOR EXPERIMENT 4: ACIDS AND BASES

In this experiment the student will design their own acid-base test for different household products. Help the student think about how they can use "controls" to determine if household products are acids or bases.

A "control" is a test they perform so they can determine what results they should expect. They should set up "control" reactions so they can know what an acid looks like with red cabbage indicator and what a base looks like with red cabbage indicator. Help them come up with their own controls.

If they get stuck, help them think through the problem with the following questions:

1. Can you name a household acid? *vinegar, lemon juice, etc.*

2. Can you name a household base? *baking soda water, ammonia*

3. What could you use for a control acid?

4. What could you use for a control base?

Direct them into discovering on their own what sorts of materials could be used for a control acid or base.

Help them set up a pH scale using household products. Have them use the acid base tables given in the chapter to create their own pH scale.

Once they have their pH scale, let them use a variety of different household products to determine the pH.

ALTERNATIVE EXPERIMENT: ACIDS AND BASES

In this chapter they learned that pH was a function of concentration. The more concentrated an acid is, the higher the pH. Ask them if they think that is true. Ask them if they could design an experiment to determine if that is true. What would they do?

If they get stuck, help them think through the problem with the following questions:

1. Do you think it is true that the pH will change when you change the concentration of an acid or base?

2. What do you think the pH of full strength ammonia is?

3. What do you think would happen to the pH if you diluted the ammonia?

4. What do you think would happen if you kept diluting the ammonia?

5. Do you think you could ever turn the ammonia solution pink? [let them try].

Experiment 4: Acids and Bases

Design an experiment to determine the pH of several unknown liquids.

Hints: First, using red cabbage juice as an acid/base indicator, create your own pH scale. Using controls to determine what an acid "looks like" with the cabbage indicator and what a base "looks like" with the cabbage indicator.

Approximate pH and color change for red cabbage indicator:

approximate pH	2	4	6	8	10	12
color	red	purple	violet	blue	blue-green	green

Experiment: _____*pH of household products*_____   Date: _____

Objective: _____*To determine the pH of several household products*_____

Materials List:

baking soda

distilled water

red cabbage

vinegar

clear ammonia

Experimental setup:

1. First I will determine what concentrated ammonia looks like with red cabbage indicator. This will be my "control" base.

2. Next I will determine what full strength vinegar looks like with red cabbage indicator. This will be my "control" base.

3. Now I will determine the pH of different household items.

Controls	color	pH
vinegar	pink	2
ammonia	green	12

pH of different household items:

item	color	pH

Have the students record the pH of several different household products.

ALTERNATIVE EXPERIMENT: DETERMINING PH AS A FUNCTION OF CONCENTRATION

Experiment _____ *Determining pH as a function of concentration* _____

Objective: _____ *To determine if pH is a function of concentration* _____

Materials List:

distilled water

red cabbage

vinegar

clear ammonia

Experimental setup:

1. First I will determine what concentrated ammonia looks like with red cabbage indicator. This will be my "control" base.

2. Next I will determine what full strength vinegar looks like with red cabbage indicator. This will be my "control" base.

3. Now I will dilute each acid and base and record the change in pH.

Concentration	color	estimated pH
one cup vinegar	red	2
3/4 cup vinegar +1/4 cup water		
1/2 cup vinegar +1/2 cup water		
1/4 cup vinegar + 3/4 cup water		

Concentration	color	estimated pH
one cup ammonia	green	12
3/4 cup ammonia +1/4 cup water		
1/2 cup ammonia +1/2 cup water		
1/4 cup ammonia + 3/4 cup water		

Conclusions:

help the students draw conclusions based on their results.

Text reading time .... 2 hours

Experiment time .... 2-3 hours

Suggested materials (same as Chapter 4)

    red cabbage

    distilled water

    ammonia

    vinegar

    baking soda

    eye dropper

1. 6 moles of NaOH?

2. Give the molarity of the following solutions: [recall that molarity is moles per liter (the number of moles divided by the number of liters)

   a. 0.5 M [5 moles/10 liters = 0.5 M]

   b. 0.25 M [2 moles/8 liters = 0.25 M]

   c. 2 M [6 moles/3 liters = 2 M]

   d. 5 M [5 moles/1 liter = 5 M]

3. 0.2 moles [2 M x 100 ml = 2 M x 0.1 liter = 2 moles/liter x 0.1 liter (liters cancel) = 0.2 moles]

4. 0.2 moles. (At the equivalence point the number of moles of base equals the number of moles of acid.)

5. a. strong acid and a strong base

6. c. strong acid and a weak base

7. Titration curve for 500 ml of a 1 M solution of HCl with 1 M NaOH. pH is 7.

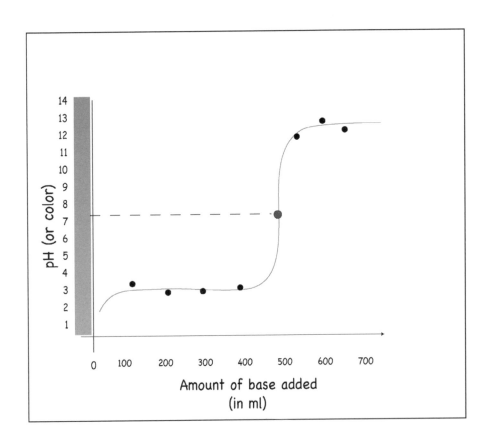

8. A general titration curve for H_2SO_4 (a strong acid) with NaOH (a strong base).

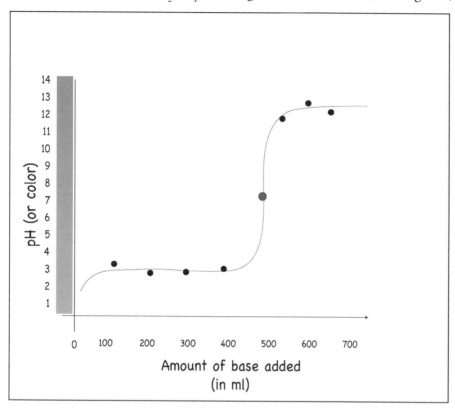

9. A general titration curve for H_3PO_4 (a polyprotic acid) titrated with NaOH (a strong base).

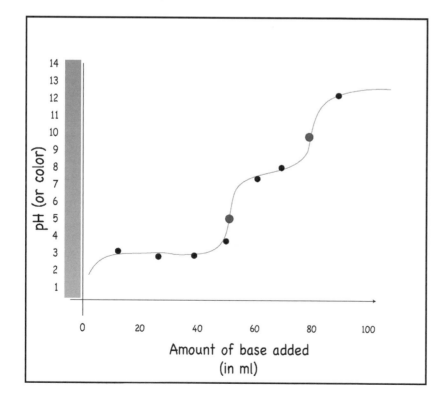

10. Draw a general titration curve for NaOH titrated with HCl.

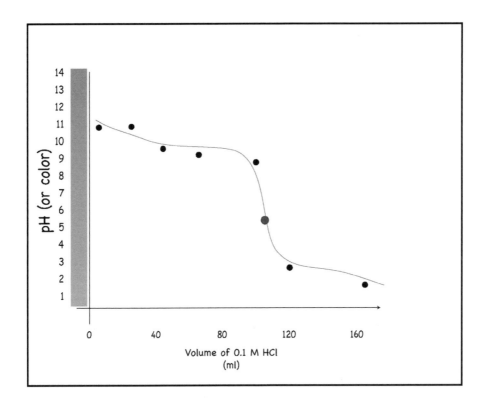

INSTRUCTIONS FOR EXPERIMENT 5: NEUTRALIZATION REACTIONS

In this experiment the student will design an experiment to determine the endpoint of a neutralization reaction, or they will try to titrate a polyprotic acid with a household base.

A. Determining an endpoint.

In order to determine the endpoint of a neutralization reaction, they need a household acid, a household base and an acid-base indicator. This experiment works well with vinegar (acetic acid) and household ammonia. Use a clear brand of ammonia as the colored brands will obscure the indicator color.

Recommend to the student that they perform the experiment using full strength ammonia and full strength acetic acid. If the experiment goes too quickly, then recommend that they dilute both the acid and the base slightly (by 1/4, then if that doesn't work by 1/3, then by 1/2 and so on.)

Before they begin their experiment, help them think through designing their experiment.

1. How can you detect the endpoint of a neutralization reaction? *using an acid base indicator*

2. At what point during the titration is the endpoint? *the moment the indicator changes color and remains changed.*

3. What would you do if the experiment proceeds too fast? *dilute the acid, base, or both and repeat.*

4. What would you do if the experiment proceeds too slow? *use a more concentrated acid, base or both and repeat.*

B. Titrating a polyprotic acid.

To titrate a polyprotic acid, a dilute base or a weak base can be used. Have the students look up polyprotic acids in the student text. Soda pop contains phosphoric acid, a polyprotic acid. The student can use any clear soda pop for this experiment.

Before they begin, help them think through their experiment with the following questions:

1. What kind of polyprotic acid will you use? *clear soda pop*

2. What kind of base will you use? *dilute ammonia or baking soda water.*

3. What sort of titration curve do you expect? *there should be two "bumps."*

Experiment 5: Neutralization Reactions

(A) Design an experiment to determine the endpoint of a neutralization reaction or
(B) Perform a titration using a polyprotic acid.

Hints: Using the pH scale from Experiment 4 draw a color scale on the y-axis with the corresponding pH for the titration. Use an acid and base that you measured the pH of in Experiment 4. Remember that concentration matters. Do not use a very dilute solution with a concentrated solution and visa versa.

Option (A) : Determining the Endpoint of a Neutralization Reaction

Experiment: *Determining the Endpoint of a Neutralization Reaction*   Date: _____

Objective: *Using an acid-base indicator, the endpoint of a neutralizatin reaction can be determined.*

Hypothesis: *The endpoint will be reached when equal amounts of ammonia and acetic acid are added*

together.

Materials List:

vinegar (acetic acid)

household ammonia (clear)

1/2 head of red cabbage (or red cabbage indicator from Chatper 4)

measuring spoons

small glass jars

Experimental setup:

1. Measure 1/2 cup of vinegar and place it into a small jar.

2. Pour 1-3 tablespoons of red cabbage indicator into the vinegar. Record the color.

3. Slowly add a tablespoon of ammonia. Record the color.

4. Continue to add ammonia one tablespoon at a time and record the color.

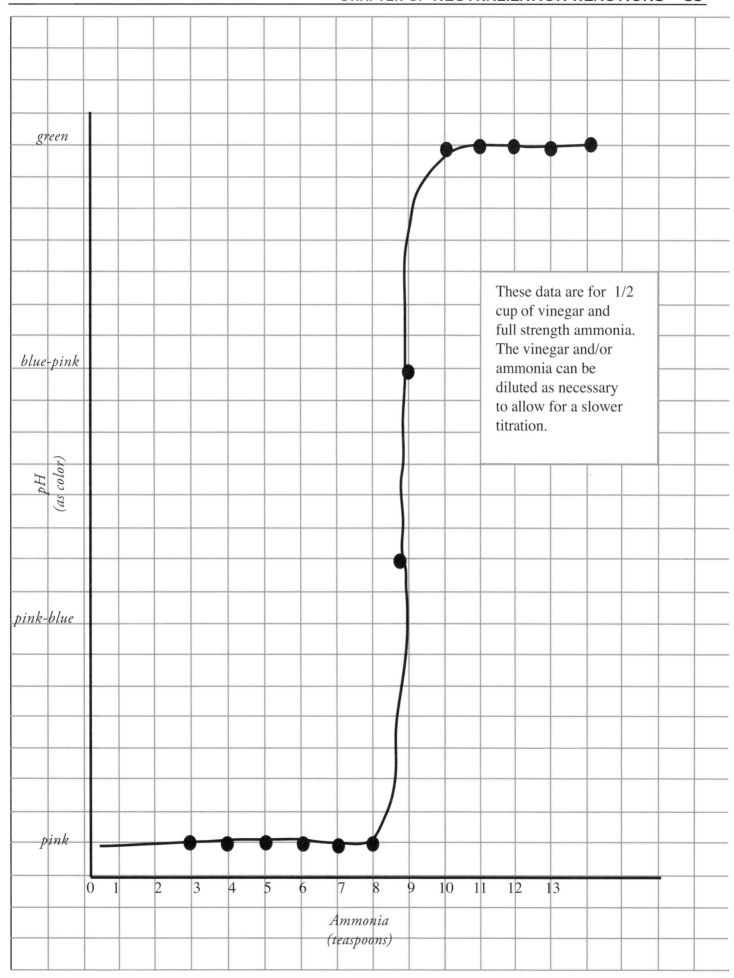

These data are for 1/2 cup of vinegar and full strength ammonia. The vinegar and/or ammonia can be diluted as necessary to allow for a slower titration.

pH (as color)

green

blue-pink

pink-blue

pink

Ammonia (teaspoons)

Option (B) : Perform a titration using a polyprotic acid

Experiment: _Titrating Soda Pop with Baking Soda_____ Date _____

Objective: _To find out if soda pop will titrate as a polyprotic acid._____

Hypothesis: _Soda pop will titrate like a polyprotic acid._____

_____

Materials List:

_clear soda pop (phosphoric acid)_____

_baking soda water [1 teaspoon baking soda + 1/2 cup of water]_____

_1/2 head of red cabbage (or red cabbage indicator from Chapter 4)_____

_measuring spoons_____

_small glass jars_____

_distilled water_____

Experimental setup:

_1. Measure 1/2 cup of soda pop and place it into a small jar._____

2. Pour 1-3 tablespoons of red cabbage indicator into the vinegar. Record the color.

_3. Slowly add a tablespoon of baking soda water. Record the color._____

4. Continue to add baking soda water one tablespoon at a time and record the color.

_____

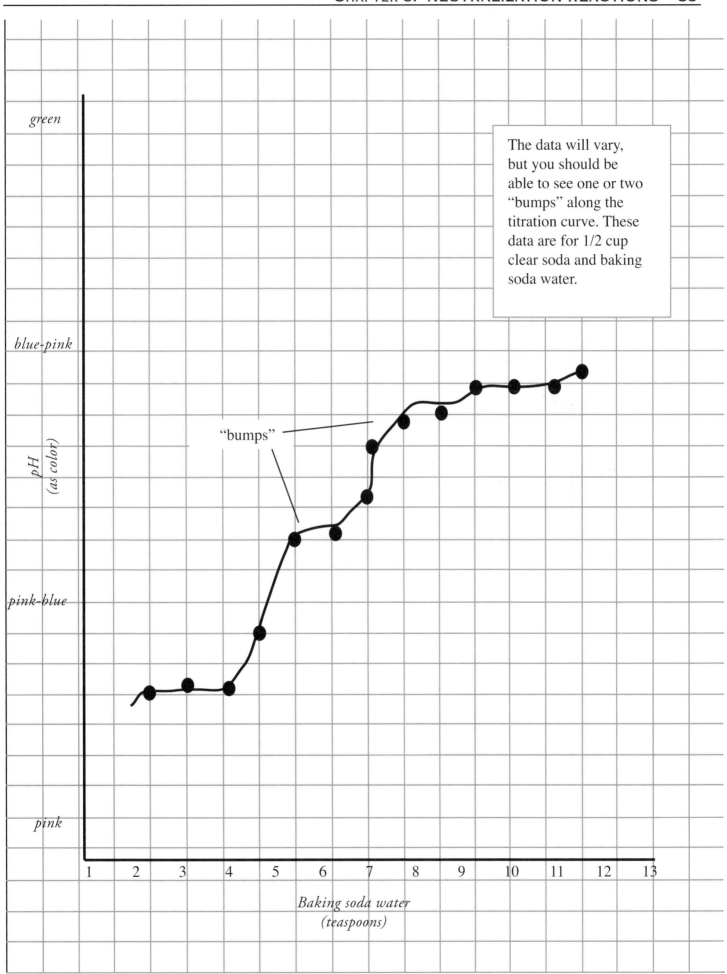

The data will vary, but you should be able to see one or two "bumps" along the titration curve. These data are for 1/2 cup clear soda and baking soda water.

"bumps"

Text reading time .... 2 hours

Experiment time .... 2-3 hours

Suggested materials :

     liquid hand-soap

     solid bar-soap

     vegetable oil

     graduated cylinder (or tall thin glass)

     ruler

     marker

     measuring spoons, measuring cup,

     3 small jars

ANSWERS TO STUDY QUESTIONS

1. A mixture is two or more substances that are physically mixed but not chemically bonded. A compound is two or more substances that are chemically bonded.

2. air, milk, ginger ale

3. water, carbon dioxide, ammonia

4. salt water

5. salad dressing

6. solid, gaseous, and liquid solutions

7. emulsions, foams, and aerosols

8. A solute is something that is dissolved into a solvent (usually of smaller quantity than the solvent). A solvent is something that a solute is dissolved into (usually of larger quantity than the solute).

9. Electronegativity is the ability of an atom to draw electrons from another atom towards itself.

10. Water is polar because oxygen is more electronegative than hydrogen and because water is bent, not linear.

INSTRUCTIONS FOR EXPERIMENT 6: TO MIX OR NOT TO MIX

The student will design an experiment to determine how well different household soaps form an emulsion.

Have the student think carefully about how they might "measure" an emulsion. Help them think through this process with the following questions:

1. What is an emulsion?

2. How can you tell where an emulsion begins and where it ends?

3. Do you think a "good" soap will make more or less of an emulsion than a "bad" soap?

4. What kinds of "controls" could you use?

Remind the students that they need to be "consistent" in their experiment. This means if they use 1 teaspoon of liquid soap of Brand A, they need to use 1 teaspoon of liquid soap of Brand B. If they use different amounts of soap and/or oil then they will not be able to compare their results.

Have the student carefully record how they will set up the experiment, how they will collect their data, and which controls they will use.

OPTIONAL: MAKING SOAP

It is also possible to have the student make their own soap using different "fats." Have the student use the Library or Internet to look up soap making techniques. They should read the entire procedure before beginning and they should be aware of any safety issues required in dealing with caustic materials, such as lye, and with cooking fats on the stove.

Internet sources:

http://millersoap.com

Experiment 6: To Mix Or Not To Mix

Design an experiment to determine how well different household soaps form an emulsion.

Hints: Use both liquid soap and hard soap. Keep your measurements the same. To measure the emulsion use a clear narrow glass or test tube and a ruler. Vary your shaking times, but once you've decided on a time to shake [1 minute, 2 minutes etc.] keep it the same throughout the rest of your experiment.

Experiment: *Testing Soap-Oil Emulsions*   **Date** _____

Objective: *To determine if liquid soap forms a better emulsion than bar soap*

Hypothesis: *Liquid soap will form a better emulsion than bar soap*

Materials List:

liquid hand-soap

solid bar-soap

vegetable oil

graduated cylinder (or tall, thin, glass container)

ruler

marker

measuring spoons, measuring cup, 3 small jars

Experimental setup:

1. crush 1/4 of a bar of regular bar soap. (note brand and ingredients)

2. mix with 1/4 cup of water to make a soap slurry.

3. take three small jars and put in the following:

jar A : 1/4 cup of water

jar B: 1/4 cup soap slurry

jar C: 1/4 cup of liquid hand soap

4. *To each jar add 1/4 cup of vegetable oil.*

5. *Cover the jars and shake vigorously for 1 minute.*

6. *Place on the table and wait 30 seconds.*

7. *Measure the size of the "emulsion" using the ruler. [The emulsion is the*

    space in between the water layer and the oil layer.]

Results:

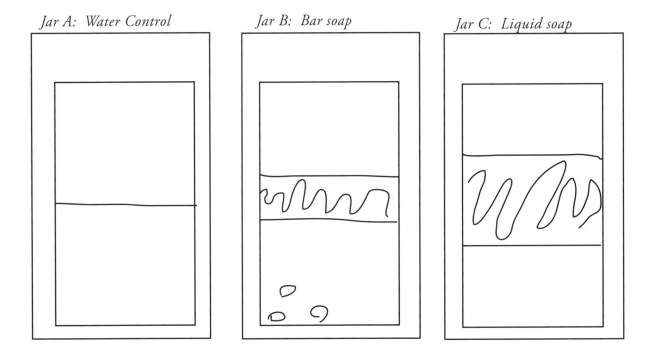

Jar A: Water control. There was no emulsion. Only small beads of oil initially trapped by the water.

Jar B: There was a small emulsion. However, not all of the soap was mixed and so it is difficult to tell how well the

  bar soap made an emulsion.

Jar C: The liquid soap made the best emulsion. Almost all of the oil was gone from the water.

Text reading time .... 2 hours

Experiment time .... 2-3 hours

Suggested materials :

    isopropanol (rubbing alcohol)

    white coffee filter paper or absorbant paper

    several flower petals and/or plant leaves

    sand

    mortar and pestle

    eye dropper

    small glass jars (6)

    scissors

ANSWERS TO STUDY QUESTIONS

1. Sand and pebbles are both solids. Grains of sand are smaller than pebbles. Pebbles and sand are made of similar materials, so their boiling point, melting point, and solubility will be similar. Filtration would be a good separation technique.

2. Sand and salt are both solids. Grains of sand and grains of salt are similar in size. Salt is water soluble, sand is not. The salt can be dissolved in water, and separated from the sand using filtration.

3. Alcohol and water are both liquids. Alcohol has a lower boiling point than water. The alcohol can be separated from the water using evaporation or distillation.

4. a. Filtration. Copper nuggets are solid, water is a liquid. The liquid will pass through the filter leaving the solid behind.

   b. Evaporation. Table salt is soluble in water, but has a much higher boiling temperature. The water will evaporate leaving the salt behind.

   c. Filtration. The table salt can be dissolved in water, and separated from the chalkdust by filtration.

   d. Extraction. If water is added to the mixture, the salt will dissolve in the water and can be extracted from the benzene. The boiling point of benzene is much lower than that of table salt, and the benzene can be evaporated off.

   e. Filtration. Egg whites react with vinegar making a solid. The egg whites can be precipitated with vinegar and then filtered from the water with a filter paper.

   f. Chromatography. Liquid or paper. The dyes will stick to the paper (or column) differently and can be separated.

   g. Filtration. The egg whites can be diluted in water and passed through a filter, separating them from the nuggets.

Challenge: The table salt and the water can be separated from the chalkdust and the nuggets using filtration. The water can be evaporated leaving the table salt. The chalkdust and the nuggets can be filtered through cheesecloth (a large pored filter) separating the chalkdust from the nuggets.

INSTRUCTIONS FOR EXPERIMENT 7: PIGMENTS IN PLANTS

The student will design an experiment to separate pigments from plant tissue.

Have the students think carefully about how they might use different solvents to separate pigments from plant tissue.   Help them think through this process with the following questions:

1. What kinds of solvents do you think plant pigments would be soluble in? [*water, vinegar, alcohol,organic solvent such as GooGone*]

2. What are some of the chemical or physical properties of plant pigments that might help with your separation? [*solubility, pH, size*]

3. From what you know of plant tissue, do you think you will have to grind or crush the plants to get the pigments out? [*yes, plant leaves often have a waxy coating that may prevent pigments from being released.*]

4. What kind of separation technique do you think would work best? [*paper chromatography*]

5. How many pigments might you expect to find in a plant leaf? [*at least two, a green and yellow band, [see below]*]

6. How many pigments might you expect to find in a flower petal?

Help the student decide how to perform the experiment with the following questions. Help them narrow the type of experiment they will perform. Their experimental set-up will vary depending on what they choose to investigate.

1. Do you want to test different solvents?
2. Do you want to test differences between leaves and petals?
3. Do you want to test differences between petals and fruits?
4. Do you want to test only green leaves?
5. Do you want to test only flower petals?
6. Do you want to test only fruit?

Plant Pigments: additional information.

Green leaves have several different kind of pigments. The most abundant pigment in land plants is chlorophyll a and lesser pigments include chorophyll b and carotenoids. The student should have some introductory knowledge of photosynthesis, but if not have the student use web or library sources for additional information. Suggested keywords: photosynthesis, chlorophyll, light energy + plants, carotenoids, electromagnetic spectrum + plants.

Flower petals have pigments called flavinoids. Flavinoids give fruits and flower petals their brilliant colors. Flavinoids can be extracted like chlorophyll a and b, and the carotenoids. For additional information about flavinoids, have the students use web or library souces. Suggested keywords: flavinoids, flower pigments, electromagnetic spectrum + plants.

Experiment 7: Pigments In Plants

Design an experiment to separate the pigments in leaves or flower petals.

Hints: Try different solvents such as rubbing alcohol, water, and a non-polar solvent such as GooGone.   Allow your solvents to interact with the leaves and flower petals for several hours or overnight, being careful not to let them evaporate.

Experiment: *Separating Plant Pigments*   Date

Objective: *Separate 2 or more pigments from a plant leaf and a flower petal using paper chromatography.*

Hypothesis: *Plant leaves will show at least two different pigments. Flower petals will show more than two pigments.*

Materials List:

isopropanol (rubbing alchohol)	*white absorbant paper*
scissors	*green leaves (2)*
sand	*flower petals (2-4)*
mortar and pestle	*eye dropper*
small glass jars (6)	

Experimental setup:

1. *Cut the leaf into small pieces with the scissors and place pieces in the mortar and pestle.*

2. *Add a small amount of sand to the cut leaves.*

3. *Grind the leaves until you have a coarse paste.*

4. *Remove mixture and place in a small glass jar.*

5. *Add (2) tablespoons of isopropanol.*

6. *Cover and let sit for 30 minutes.*

7. *Repeat steps for flower petals.*

8. *Cut the white absorbant paper into 4-6 thin strips (1" wide, 4"-5" in length).*

9. Take the eye dropper and place several small drops of the leaf extract onto two of the 4 strips. [two strips are used instead of one in case one sample does not work] On the other two strips, add drops of the flower petal extract. Add several drops of each extract to each strip.

10. Place 1/4 cup of isopropanol in four of the small glass jars.

11. Label the jar accordingly [two for "leaf extract" and two for "flower extract."]

12. Tape the edge of the paper strips to the pencil. Dip the other end of the paper strip into the isopropanol in one of the four jars. Repeat, with each strip in a separate jar.

13. Allow the solvent [isopropanol] to migrate up the paper strips overnight.

14. Record your results below.

NOTE : Have the students tape the strips of paper onto their worksheet.

Results:

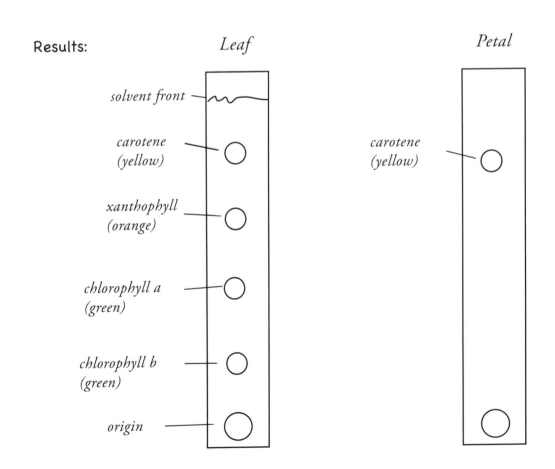

Leaf / Petal

solvent front

carotene (yellow)

xanthophyll (orange)

chlorophyll a (green)

chlorophyll b (green)

origin

Conclusions:

The student should notice a difference between the chromatograms for the green leaf and the flower petals. The green leaf will contain both chlorophyll a and chlorophyll b and be visible as green spots on the chromatogram. The flower petals probably will not. Both may contain yellow and orange pigments.

For future study:

Encourage the student to investigate plant pigments from library or web resources.

Have them think about the following:

1. *Are there other solvents you might have used? [acetone]*

2. *Do you think you might have seen different pigments? [perhaps, not all pigments are soluble in the same solvents].*

3. *What kinds of pigments do you think you might find in an orange? or an apple?*

4. *What do you think would happen if you used a different kind of paper?*

5. *What other ways could you separate plant pigments? [column chromatography]*

Text reading time .... 2 hours

Experiment time .... 2-3 hours

Suggested materials :

      tincture of iodine

      brown paper bag

      marking pen

      sugar

      potatoes

      other foods such as:

            bread, fruit, pasta, butter, etc.

ANSWERS TO STUDY QUESTIONS: PART A

1. Organic compounds are carbon-containing and inorganic compounds generally do not contain carbon. Some exceptions are carbon dioxide, some carbon containing acids and pure carbon compounds like diamonds or graphite.

2. alkanes, alkenes, and alkynes. Alkanes have single bonds, alkenes have double bonds and alkynes have triple bonds.

3.

4. A carbon atom double bonded to an oxygen atom and also single bonded to an -OH group.

$$\begin{array}{c} O \\ \| \\ -C-OH \end{array}$$

5. A carbon that is single bonded to an oxygen and the oxygen is single bonded to another carbon.

$$-C-O-C-$$

ANSWERS TO STUDY QUESTIONS: PART B

1. Living things are different than non-living things because living things reproduce themselves, may be able to move, require nutrients for living and can cease to be living, i.e. dead.

2. minerals (from meat, vegetables, etc.); vitamins (vegetables, eggs, fish etc.) , and carbohydrates (bread, pasta etc.).

3. gluconeogenesis and photosynthesis.

4. amylose and amylopectin

5. A saturated fat does not have any double bonds in the carbon chain, and an unsaurated fat contains one or more double bonds in the carbon chain.

INSTRUCTIONS FOR EXPERIMENT 8: TESTING FOOD FOR CARBOHYDRATES AND LIPIDS

The students will design an experiment to determine if a variety of foods contain carbohydrates and/or lipids (fats).

Background:

Carbohydrates can be detected easily with an iodine solution. Most drugstores carry "tincture of iodine" which contains iodine and alcohol which can be used for this experiment. Iodine specifically detects polysaccharides, and will not pick up mono or discaccharides.

Lipids can be detected using a simple brown paper bag. Lipids will leave a translucent spot on a brown paper bag.

Help your student design their experiment. Have the students do some internet or library research before beginning their experiment. Help direct them with the following questions:

1. How do you detect carbohydrates in a sample? [*tincture of iodine detects carbohydrates*]

2. Which carbohydrates will iodine detect? [*polysaccharides*]

3. How will you know your test is working? [*use control samples*]

4. What kinds of "controls" could you use? [*a "positive" control (starch water from a potato) and a negative control (water). For the lipid use water as a negative control.*]

5. How can you detect lipids? [*using a brown paper bag*]

6. How could you measure the amount of lipid? [*measuring the lipid spot as a function of time*].

Have the students test a variety of foods.

Foods with carbohydrates include:
    bread
    pasta
    potatoes
    unripened fruit such as bananas, apples, etc.

Foods that contain lipids include:
    butter
    oil
    cheese
    cream

Experiment 8: Testing food for Carbohydrates and Lipids

Design an experiment to test different foods for the presence of carbohydrates and lipids.

You will need iodine and a brown paper sack.

Iodine reacts with carbohydrates turning them black. Iodine is very poisonous – DO NOT EAT
Lipids will make a brown paper sack translucent (clear).

Hints: First perform some "control" reactions.

Experiment: *Testing Cheese and Bread*   Date _____

Objective: *To determine if cheese and potatoes contain both carbohydrates and lipids*

Hypothesis: *Cheese will contain only lipids and bread (without butter) will contain only carbohydrates*

Materials List:

brown paper sack

tincture of iodine

marking pen

one raw potato

water

one piece of yellow cheese and one piece of bread

Experimental setup:

1. *Controls will first be set up to determine what a positive and negative outcome will look like.*

2. *Positive Control for Carboydrate: cut the raw potato into cubes and place in 1/2 cup of warm water.*

   Allow the potato to sit for 10 minutes. Drain off the potato juice. This water contains potato starch.

   Add 1 drop of iodine to the water and observe. The water should turn black.

3. *Negative Control for Carboydrate. Add 1 drop of iodine to 1/4 cup of warm water.*

   The solution should not turn black, but stay clear or turn slightly brown.

4. *Positive Control for Lipids. Take a small dab of butter and place it on a piece of brown paper sack. Let the butter sit for 10 minutes. Wipe excess butter and place brown paper sack under a bright light. Look for a translucent spot.*

5. *Negative Control for Lipids. Take a small drop of water and place on a piece of brown paper sack. Let the water sit for 10 minutes. Wipe excess water away and place brown paper sack under a bright light. There should be no translucent spot remaining.*

6. *Now test the bread and cheese for carbohydrates and lipids.*

7. *Divide cheese into two pieces. To one piece add a drop of iodine. Place the other piece on the brown paper sack. Allow the cheese to sit 10 minutes.*

8. *Divide the bread into two pieces. To one piece add a drop of iodine. Place the other piece on the brown paper sack. Allow the bread to sit for 10 minutes.*

9. *Record results below.*

Results

food item	carbohydrates	lipids
Control water	--	--
Control potato water	+ +	--
Control butter	--	+ +
cheese	--	+ +
bread	+ +	--

Conclusions:

The cheese contained only lipids and not carbohydrates. The bread contained only carbohydrates and not lipids.

Text reading time .... 2 hours

Experiment time .... 2-3 hours

Suggested materials :

Elmer's® white glue

Borax

small jars or paper cups

distilled water

ANSWERS TO STUDY QUESTIONS

1. polyethylene

2. Kevlar

3. structure of the polymer and the way the polymer chains pack with each other

4. polystyrene

5. Nylon or Dacron

6. natural rubber

7. a "dangling bond" or an electron that is not bonded

8. An intitator free radical is used to start the process of chain formation by creating free radicals on individual monomers.

9. HDPE - High Density Polyethylene; LDPE- Low Density Polyethylene. HDPE has fewer branching than LDPE and so it packs together more tightly making HDPE harder and tougher than LDPE.

10. A condensation reaction takes two monomers that chemically react to form a new molecule giving off a by-product such as water. In an addition reaction the monomers simply add, one to another, without producing water as a by-product.

INSTRUCTIONS FOR EXPERIMENT 9: CROSSLINKING POLYMERS

In this experiment the student will try to determine how the polymer properties change as a function of crosslinking. Elmer's glue is a polymer made of polyvinylacetate (PVA). Have the student research the chemical composition of Elmer's glue using the internet or library. Students can also write to the company that makes Elmer's glue to request information about their product. Borax, found in laundry starch, causes PVA to form crosslinks with itself. As a result, the physical properties of Elmer's glue change and can be easily observed.

Help the student think about how to design an experiment to determine how well Borax cross-links Elmer's glue. A sample experiment is given below.

Experiment 9: Crosslinking Polymers

Design an experiment to test how polymer properties change as a function of crosslinking

Hints: You know that Elmer's glue and Borax make a polymer. Determine what happens if you add different amounts of Borax to the Elmer's glue. Keeping the amount of glue consistent, vary the concentration of the borax. Observe the polymer properties as a function of Borax concentration.

Experiment: *Crosslinking Elmer's glue with borax*   Date _____

Objective: *To observe the changes in physical properties of Elmer's glue as a function of Borax*

concentration.

Hypothesis: *Elmer's glue will become harder and less sticky with more Borax*

Materials List:

Elmer's glue

Borax

Distilled water

(9) small jars or paper cups

Experimental setup:

1. *Make (4) different mixtures of Borax and water at different Borax concentrations (amount of*

Borax per given volume of water) and label them A, B, C, and D.

A- 1 teaspoon Borax in 1/4 cup of distilled water.

B - 2 teaspoons of Borax in 1/4 cup of distilled water.

C - 3 teaspoons of Borax in 1/4 cup of distilled water.

D - 4 teaspoons of Borax in 1/4 cup of distilled water.

2. Add 1/4 cup of Elmer's glue to (5) small jars or paper cups. Make sure the amount of Elmer's glue in each cup is roughly the same.

3. Label the jars or cups, A, B, C, D and E.

4. To the cup labeled E, add 1/4 of distilled water. Mix the glue and water for several minutes and record the results below. This is a "negative control" - i.e. what happens to the glue if no borax is added.

5. To the cup labeled A, add the 1/4 cup of borax and distilled water. Mix the glue and borax mixture for several minutes. Record the results below.

6. Repeat step 5 for the jars labeled B, C, and D.

Results:

®Jar	Amount Borax (tsp)	Observations
A	1	the glue did not show any significant changes in physical properties
B	2	the glue started to get slightly stringy.
C	3	the glue was more stringy and became rubbery.
D	4	the glue became rubbery and stiffer over time.
E	0	the glue did not show any changes in physical properties, it only became more dilute.

Conclusions:

The negative control of water and glue showed no changes in physical properties. As the Borax concentration was increased, the glue became stringy and rubbery. This shows that the Borax crosslinks the PVA polymers in the glue and as a result changes the glue's physical properties.

NOTE: This is a sample experiment - your results may vary.

Text reading time .... 2 hours

Experiment time .... 2-3 hours

Suggested materials :

    1 large onion

    1 large egg

    sieve

    distilled water

    meat tenderizer

    liquid detergent

    small jars or test tubes (2)

    wooden stick or Q-tip

    70% - 90% rubbing alcohol (isopropanol)

OPTIONAL KIT:

EXTRACTING FRUIT AND VEGETABLE DNA

DNA DEPOT

WWW.DNADEPOT.COM

1. Isoleucine

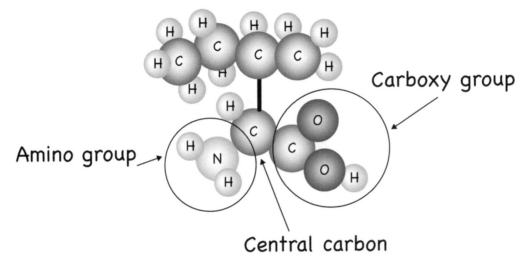

Carboxy group

Amino group

Central carbon

2. Tyrosine and Glycine

Tyrosine

N-terminus

peptide bond

Glycine

C-terminus

3. The primary structure of a protein describes the sequence of amino acids on the polypeptide chain. So for example the primary structure of a small polypeptide might be: Arginine - Glycine - Tryptophan - Alanine (R-G-W-A).

4. The secondary structure of a protein describes how the polypeptide chain folds up. A helix is an example of a protein secondary structure.

5. The tertiary structure determines the overall shape of a protein. A domain is an example of a tertiary structure.

6. The quaternary structure of a protein describes two or more polypeptide chains functioning together. Hemoglobin has four polypeptide chains nested together to form the quaternary structure.

7. Adenine, Thymine, Cytosine, and Guanine.

8. Adenine, Uracil, Cytosine, and Guanine.

9. Using the abbreviated codon set below, write a corresponding amino acid sequence for the following DNA sequence: ATGCCTGATTTCGGA.

First - divide the sequence starting with the first letter into groups of three letters:

ATG-CCT-GAT-TTC-GGA.

Next - convert all of the "T's" to "U's" [for RNA].

AUG-CCU-GAU-UUC-GGA.

Finally - look at the chart below and write out the amino acid sequence for the DNA sequence above:

Alanine	Glutamic acid	Glycine	Asparagine	Methionine	Proline	Phenylalanine
CGA	GAA	GGA	GAU	AUG	CCU	UUC

Methionine- Proline - Asparagine - Phenylanlanine - Glycine

10. RNA polymerase reads the DNA strand and makes a corresponding polymer of RNA.

INSTRUCTIONS FOR EXPERIMENT 10: DNA EXTRACTION

In this experiment the student will try to determine which has more DNA, an egg or an onion. Have the student first read the Extraction Protocol found at the end of the Laboratory notebook. They should read through the protocol carefully and address any questions they may have before starting the experiment.

Have the student guess which will have more DNA and onion or an egg. Have them think about the following questions:

1. How many cells do you think are in an egg? *one, the egg is a single cell.*

2. How many cells do you think are in an onion? *many, the onion has many layers of cells.*

3. Which cells are larger, an onion or an egg? *the egg cell is much larger*

4. Which cells do you think would have more DNA? Why?

When they have read the extraction protocol and have had a chance to think about the experiment, help them formulate a hypothesis for the experiment. Which do they think would have more DNA?

Have them follow the protocol for both the egg and the onion, pulling out DNA. Help them write out the steps for extracting DNA from the onion and from the egg.

They should discover that although an egg cell is much larger than an onion cell, because DNA is in each cell, the onion will have more DNA. They will not be able to pull out DNA from an egg because it is only a single cell and therefore the amount of DNA they can extract it is too small to be seen. However, they should get plenty of DNA from an onion.

Help them discuss any errors or problems they may have encountered during the process.

Experiment 10: Which has more DNA? An onion or an egg?

In this experiment you will extract DNA from an onion and an egg and compare which has more DNA.

Hint: Follow the protocol for extracting DNA from food items. Try to be consistent with your measurements. Try not to lose too much of your experiment as you transfer your products from container to container.

Experiment: *Which has more DNA? An Onion or an Egg?* _____ Date _____

Objective: *To determine if an onion or an egg has more DNA*

Hypothesis: *An egg will have more DNA than an onion*

Materials List:

1 large onion

1 large egg

sieve

distilled water

meat tenderizer

liquid detergent

small jars or test tubes (2)

wooden stick or Q-tip

70% - 90% rubbing alcohol (isopropanol)

Experimental setup:

see DNA extraction protocol

Conclusions:

The student will discover that an onion has more DNA than a single egg. Help them think about why this is true. If they did not get this result, ask them what problems they may have encountered and how they might fix them. Also ask them to discuss their sources of error.

REFERENCES	

Lesson Summary: _DNA extraction_

This protocol describes a simple method for extracting DNA from living tissues.

Commentary:

This is a generalized protocol taken from a variety of references. It describes the general steps and rationale for nucleic acid extraction. The steps can be adapted to a particular sample by adjusting the volumes, and/or using a variety of different materials.

There are three overall steps for extracting nucleic acids from living tissues.

Step 1: Lysing the cells in the sample
Step 2: Separating the nucleic acids from the cell material
Step 3: Pulling out the nucleic acids.

Step 1: Lysing the cells in the sample

Recall that living tissues are made of cells and the nucleic acids are on the insides of cells. In order to extract nucleic acids from cells, the cells need to be opened, or _lysed_. The first step of the protocol opens, or lysis, the cells. This is accomplished by using a combination of detergents and enzymes (found in meat tenderizer, for use on animal cells.)

Step 2: Separating the DNA from the cell material

Once the cells are lysed, or broken open, there is a mixture of DNA, RNA, proteins, and other cell parts. The DNA and RNA needs to be separated from the proteins and other cell parts. This is accomplished in Step 2 by using alcohol. The nucleic acids are not soluable in the alcohol, so they precipitate out of the solution.

Step 3: Pulling out the DNA

After the DNA is separated from the cells parts, it can be extracted, or pulled out of the solution. This is accomplished in Step 3 using a wooden stick or Q-tip. Although all nucleic acids can be removed, only DNA survives the procedure. RNA is chewed up, or degraded, during the process by enzymes. DNA is more robust that RNA and is not easily degraded by enzymes.

MATERIALS

- *Suggested Samples*

The sample can be any living thing including but not limited to:

vegetable tissue, such as spinach, peas, green beans, broccoli, onions etc.

grains such as wheat germ, corn, oatmeal, seeds, or yeast

animal tissue such as eggs, chicken or beef livers, chicken hearts, etc.

- *Detergents (Liquid)*

Try any of the following:

- *Rubbing alcohol (isopropanol)*

- *Wooden stir stick or Q-tip*

- *Coffee filter*

- *Table salt*

STEP I

LYSING THE SAMPLE

Part A: Prepare the sample for lysis

Put your sample in a blender and add twice as much cold water as sample [so for 1 cup of peas, add two cups of water], 1 teaspoon of table salt, and blend the sample on high speed until the sample is pureed [about 15 - 20 seconds].

Next pour your sample through a strainer or sieve into a glass jar or large test tube. This separates the larger plant or animal tissue from the cells. You should start with at least 1/4 cup of liquid.

Part B : Lysis

Add detergent to the cells to break them open. Use (1) tablespoon of detergent per cup of cell mixture. If you are lysing animal cells, add an additional teaspoon of meat tenderizer. Gently swirl the cell, water, detergent and meat tenderizer mixture being careful not to create foam. Allow the mixture to sit for 5 minutes gently swirling intermittently.

STEP 2

SEPARATING THE DNA FROM THE CELL MATERIAL

Next, tilting the jar or test tube, slowly add 1/4 cup of isopropanol per 1/4 cup of the cell-water mixture, pouring it down the inside of the jar or test tube. The alcohol will float to the top of the jar or test tube and the DNA will precipitate at the water-alcohol interface [the place where the alcohol and water meet]. This needs to be done slowly without agitating the mixture.

STEP 3

PULLING OUT THE DNA

Take the Q-tip or wooden stick and insert it into the alcohol layer. Gently touch the alcohol-water interface and swirl the stick or Q-tip pulling up slightly. The DNA will collect on the stick or Q-tip and there should be long strands visible. Continue spinning and collecting the DNA for a few seconds. Pull out the stick and place the DNA on a coffee filter to dry.

Troubleshooting is part of science. Almost no experiment works the first time. Many new discoveries are made by scientists when their experiments "fail."

TROUBLESHOOTING

FREQUENTLY ASKED QUESTIONS

What if I do not get at least 1/4 cup of liquid from Step 1, Part A, should I continue?

No. If you do not get at least 1/4 cup of material from Step 1 Part A blend the sample again adding more water. With smaller volumes, there may not be enough DNA extracted to visualize.

What if I do not see an alcohol-water inerface?

If you do not see an alcohol-water interface try adding more alcohol being careful not to agitate the sample. If you still do not see an interface, check the concentration of your alcohol and make sure it is not less than 70% alcohol. If your alcohol is more than 70% and you still do not see an interface, add twice the volume of alcohol to sample. You should eventually see an interface. If this fails, discard the sample and start over making sure you use water in Step 1.

What if I see foam?

Carefully remove the foam with an eyedropper without agitating the sample.

What if I do not get any DNA?

There could be several reasons you do not see any DNA.

1) You did not use enough starting material. Repeat the experiment and double the amount of starting material.

2) You did not use enough detergent. Repeat the experiment using more detergent.

3) You did not use the right kind of detergent. Repeat the experiment with a different detergent.

4) You did not let the sample sit long enough to break open the cells. Repeat the experiment and allow the sample to sit for a longer period of time.

5) You did not add detergent or enzyme to the sample. Repeat experiment adding enzyme or detergent or both.

6) You did not add enough alcohol. Add more alcohol.

7) The alcohol you added was not concentrated enough. Add 70-90% rubbing alcohol.

8) There is not enough salt in the water mixture to precipitate the sample. Add 1 teaspoon of table salt to your water-cell-alcohol mixture. Swirl. Add more rubbing alcohol until you see an interface and try to pull out the DNA.

DNA EXTRACTION

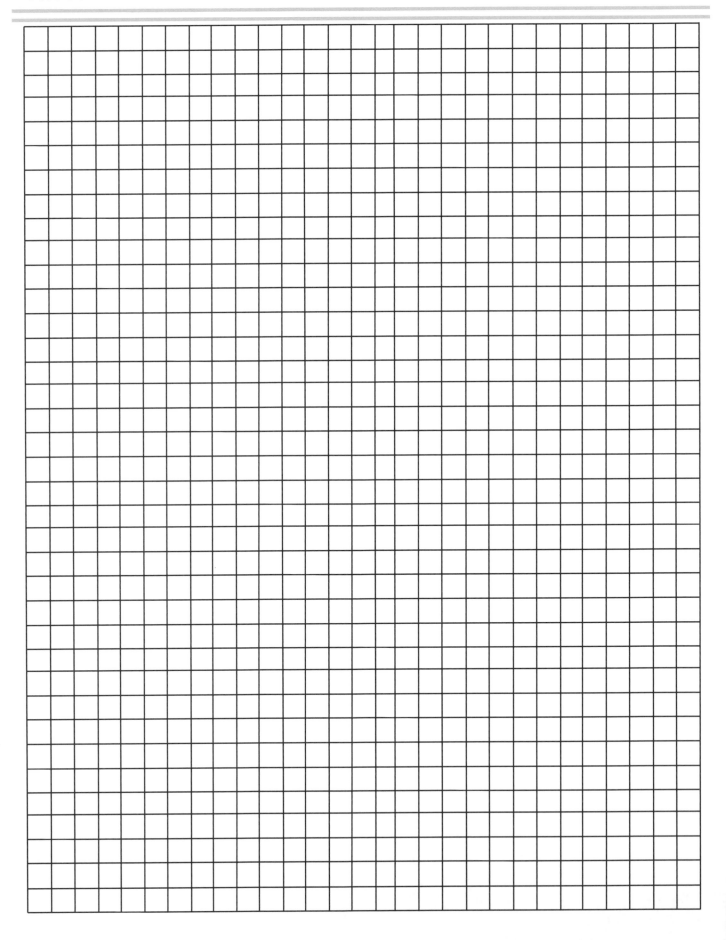

DNA EXTRACTION

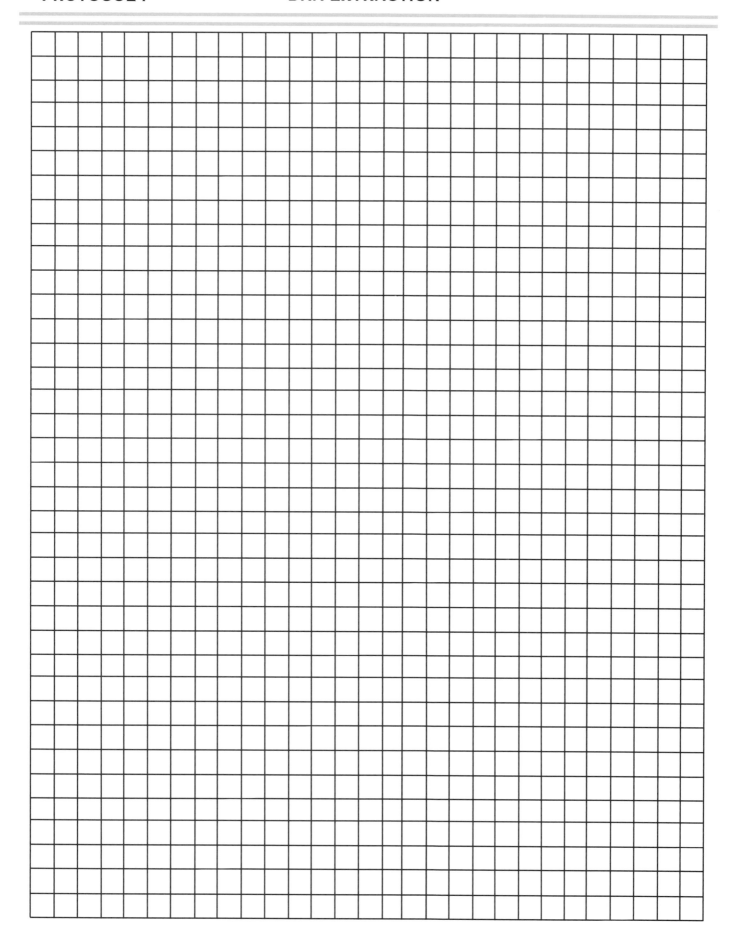

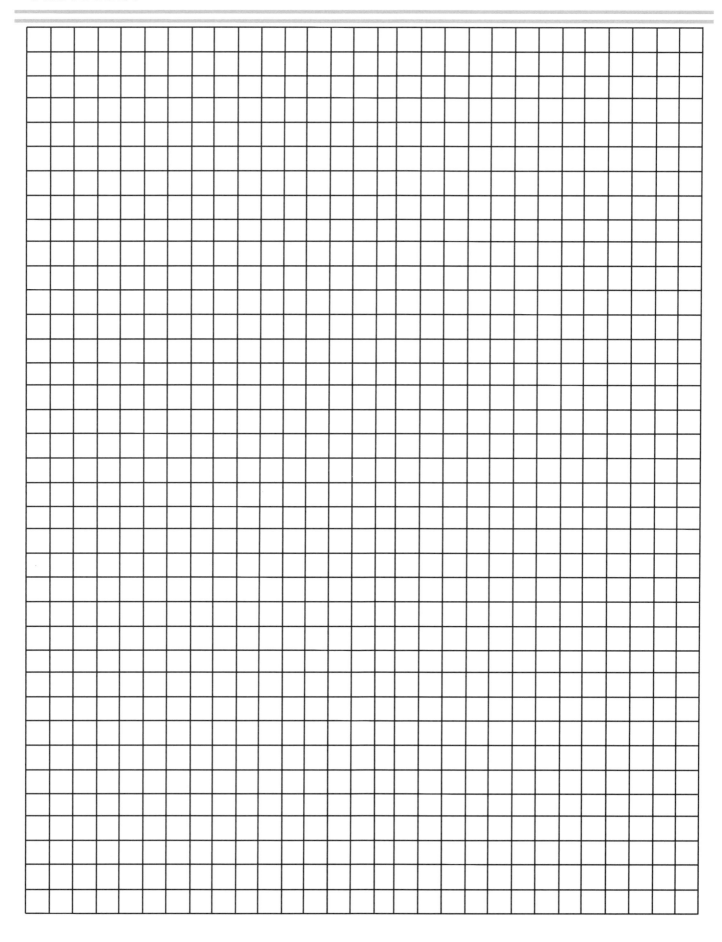

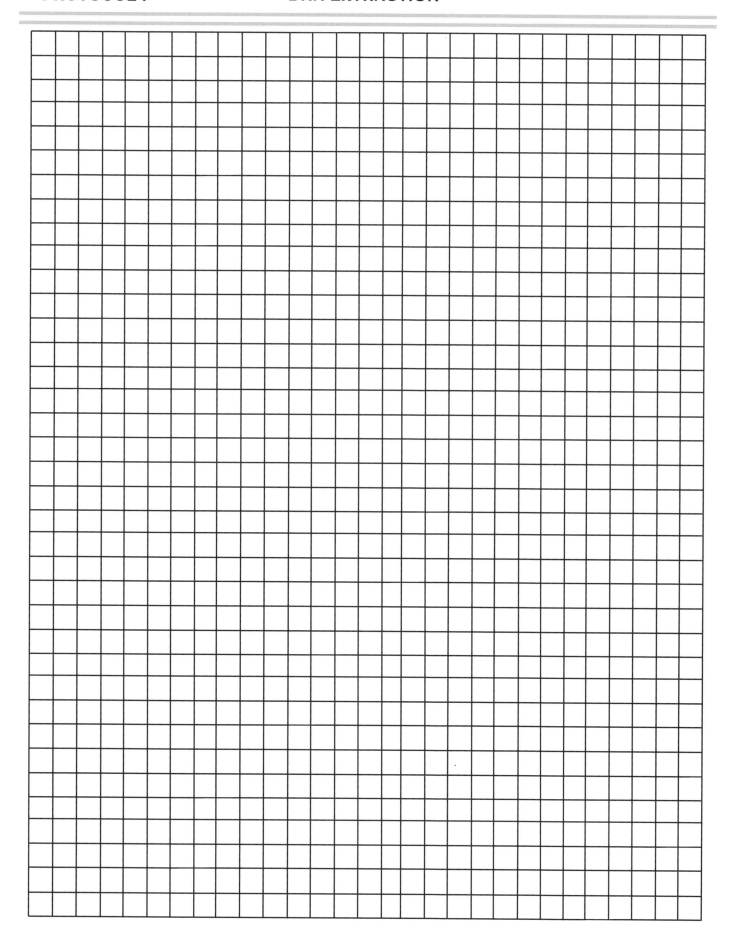

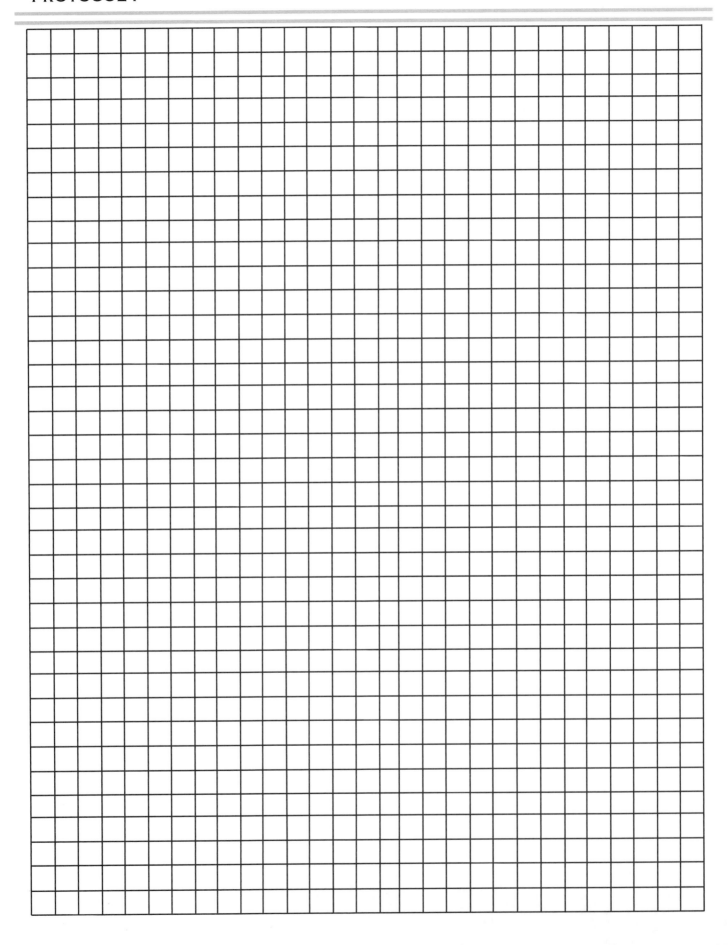

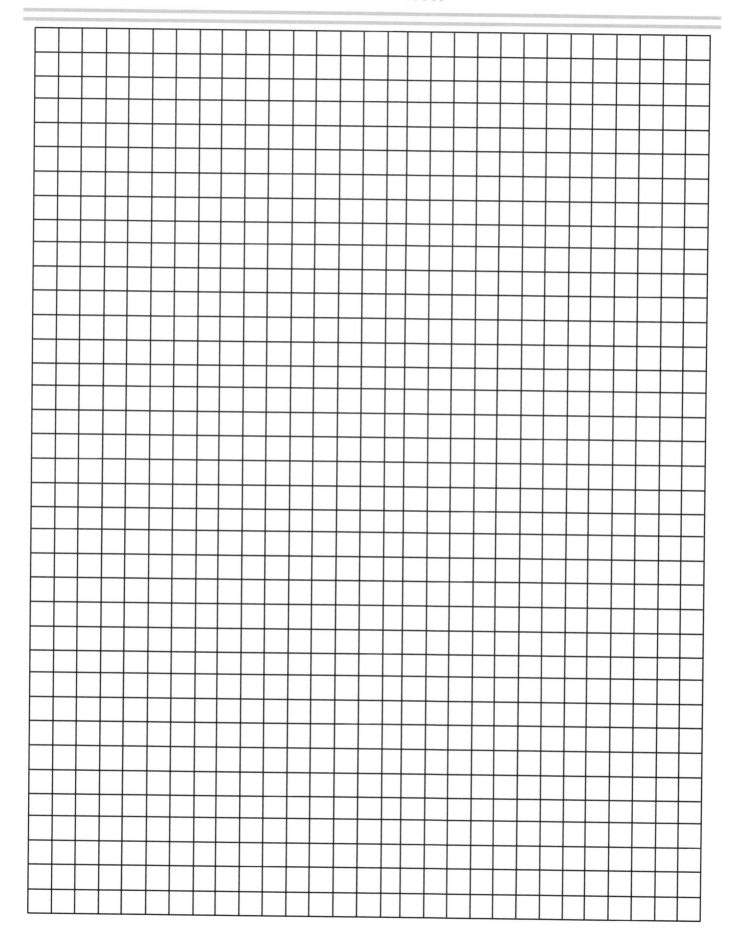

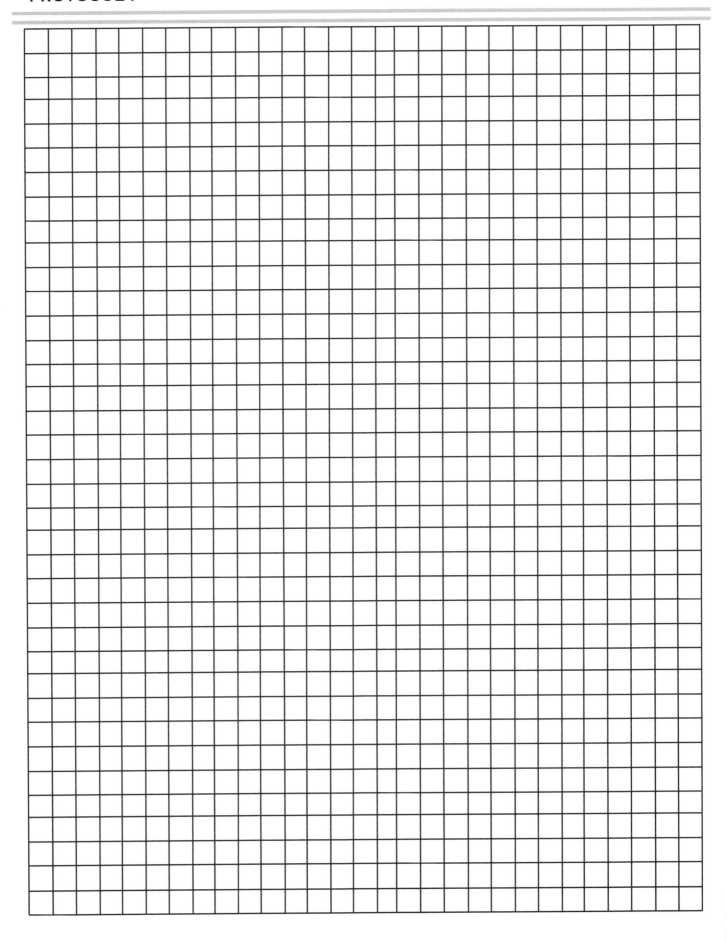

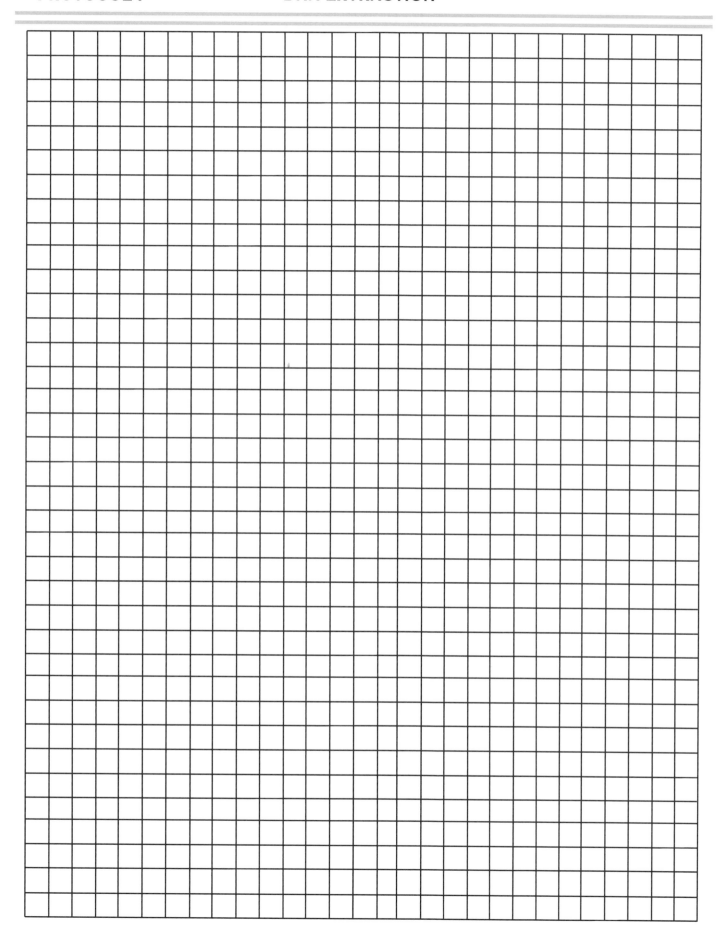

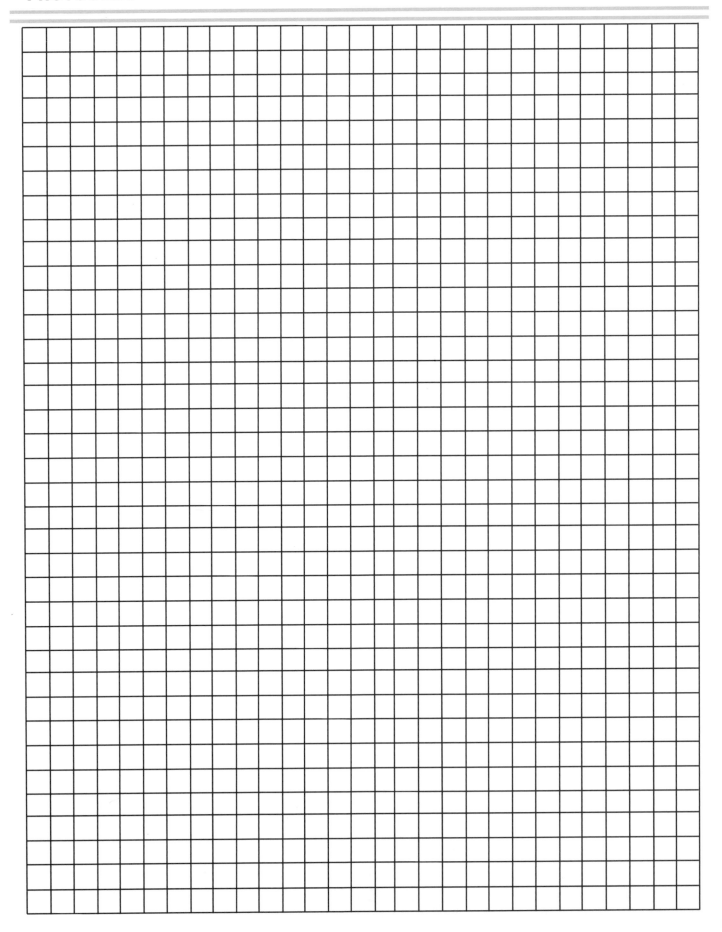